Unlocking the Secrets of Science

Profiling 20th Century Achievers in Science, Medicine, and Technology

Christiaan Barnard and the Story of the First Successful Heart Transplant

John Bankston

PO Box 619
Bear, Delaware 19701

Unlocking the Secrets of Science

Profiling 20th Century Achievers in Science, Medicine, and Technology

Luis Alvarez and the Development of the Bubble Chamber
Marc Andreessen and the Development of the Web Browser
Oswald Avery and the Story of DNA
Frederick Banting and the Discovery of Insulin
Christiaan Barnard and the Story of the First Successful Heart Transplant
Tim Berners-Lee and the Development of the World Wide Web
Chester Carlson and the Development of Xerography
Wallace Carothers and the Story of DuPont Nylon
Francis Crick and James Watson: Pioneers in DNA Research
Jacques-Yves Cousteau: His Story Under the Sea
Raymond Damadian and the Development of the MRI
Gerhard Domagk and the Discovery of Sulfa
Paul Ehrlich and Modern Drug Development
Albert Einstein and the Theory of Relativity
Willem Einthoven and the Story of Electrocardiography
Philo T. Farnsworth: The Life of Television's Forgotten Inventor
Enrico Fermi and the Nuclear Reactor
Alexander Fleming and the Story of Penicillin
Henry Ford and the Assembly Line
Robert Goddard and the Liquid Rocket Engine
Otto Hahn and the Story of Nuclear Fission
William Hewlett: Pioneer of the Computer Age
Godfrey Hounsfield and the Invention of CAT Scans
Edwin Hubble and the Theory of the Expanding Universe
Robert Jarvik and the First Artificial Heart
Willem Kolff and the Invention of the Dialysis Machine
Barbara McClintock: Pioneering Geneticist
Lise Meitner and the Atomic Age
Joseph E. Murray and the Story of the First Human Kidney Transplant
Linus Pauling and the Chemical Bond
John R. Pierce: Pioneer in Satellite Communications
Charles Richter and the Story of the Richter Scale
Sally Ride: The Story of the First American Female in Space
Edward Roberts and the Story of the Personal Computer
Wilhelm Roentgen and the Discovery of X Rays
Jonas Salk and the Polio Vaccine
Edward Teller and the Development of the Hydrogen Bomb
Selman Waksman and the Discovery of Streptomycin
Robert A. Weinberg and the Search for the Cause of Cancer
Stephen Wozniak and the Story of Apple Computer

Christiaan Barnard and the Story of the First Successful Heart Transplant

Copyright © 2003 by Mitchell Lane Publishers, Inc. All rights reserved. No part of this book may be reproduced without written permission from the publisher. Printed and bound in the United States of America.

Printing   2   3   4   5   6   7   8   9

Library of Congress Cataloging-in-Publication Data

Bankston, John, 1974-
    Christiaan Barnard and the story of the first successful heart transplant/John Bankston.
        p. cm — (Unlocking the secrets of science)
    Summary: Introduces the surgeon who in 1967 became the first to successfully transplant a donor heart into another human being.
    Includes bibliographical references and index.
    ISBN 1-58415-120-X (lib. bndg.)

    1. Barnard, Christiaan, 1922- 2. Transplant surgeons—South Africa—Biography—Juvenile literature. 3. Heart—Transplantation—Juvenile literature. [1. Barnard, Christiaan, 1922- 2. Physicians. 3. Heart—Transplantation. 4. Transplantation of organs, tissues, etc.] I. Title. II. Series.
    RD27.35.B365 B36 2002   2002023615

921
BAR

ABOUT THE AUTHOR: Born in Boston, Massachusetts, John Bankston began publishing articles in newspapers and magazines while still a teenager. Since then, he has written over two hundred articles, and contributed chapters to books such as *Crimes of Passion* and *Death Row 2000*, which have been sold in bookstores around the world. He has recently written a number of biographies for Mitchell Lane including books on Mandy Moore, Jessica Simpson and Jonas Salk. He currently lives in Los Angeles, California, pursuing a career in the entertainment industry. He has worked as a writer for the movies Dot-Com and the upcoming *Planetary Suicide*, which begins filming in 2002. As an actor John has appeared in episodes of *Sabrina the Teenage Witch*, *Charmed* and *Get Real* along with appearances in the films *Boys and Girls*, and *America So Beautiful*. He has a supporting part in *Planetary Suicide* and has recently completed his first young adult novel, *18 To Look Younger*.

PUBLISHER'S NOTE: In selecting those persons to be profiled in this series, we first attempted to identify the most notable accomplishments of the 20th century in science, medicine, and technology. When we were done, we noted a serious deficiency in the inclusion of women. For the greater part of the 20th century science, medicine, and technology were male-dominated fields. In many cases, the contributions of women went unrecognized. Women have tried for years to be included in these areas, and in many cases, women worked side by side with men who took credit for their ideas and discoveries. Even as we move forward into the 21st century, we find women still sadly underrepresented. It is not an oversight, therefore, that we profiled mostly male achievers. Information simply does not exist to include a fair selection of women.

Contents

Chapter 1
Taking a Risk   7

Chapter 2
A Rural Childhood   13

Chapter 3
Some Lucky Failings   21

Chapter 4
Getting to the Heart of It   27

Chapter 5
The Operation   33

Chapter 6
Fame!   41

Chronology   44

Timeline of Discovery   45

Glossary of Terms   46

Further Reading   46

Index   48

South African surgeon, Dr. Christiaan Barnard was a pioneer in heart transplantation. He had the courage to risk failure and the perseverance to continue even when he was not successful.

Chapter 1

Taking a Risk

Many heroes and heroines of science achieved greatness through their discoveries. They uncovered a scientific principle, found the cure for a dread disease, or invented a new technology. Other scientists and doctors became well known when they combined the work of others in a new way. These include scientists such as Edward Teller, who brought together others' theories in order to develop the hydrogen bomb, and doctors such as Frederick Banting, discoverer of insulin, who used previously published studies in his quest to find a cure for diabetes.

Yet not every advance in the world of science or medicine has occurred because of a discovery, or even because someone combined previous theories. Some scientists have received recognition not through innovation, but because they were willing to take risks when those around them lacked the courage to do so. The story of the world's first heart transplant is an example of this type of courage.

The heart is a hollow organ, beating an average of sixty to one hundred times per minute when healthy and at rest. In one year the human heart can beat over 30 million times— 2 billion times in an average life span. This action drives blood through the blood vessels, from the thick arteries to the smaller veins and tiny capillaries. These blood vessels are like the body's highway system. The blood cells are like delivery trucks transporting oxygen from the lungs and returning with waste: carbon dioxide that is exhaled, or breathed out, from the lungs. They also transport nutrients from the digestive system.

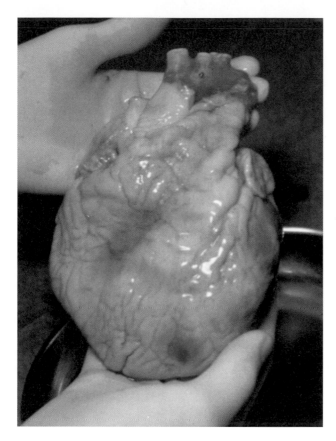

A surgeon's gloved hands hold a freshly removed human heart during a heart transplant. The heart is a muscular organ in the chest that pumps blood around the body.

The heart lies close to the center of the chest, just between the lungs. Most people think they are placing their hand over it when their fingertips are just above the lower left portion. This is the section of the heart you can feel beating.

Within its four chambers—the upper two called the atria and the lower two called the ventricles—the heart is a more efficient machine than any ever invented by man. Yet when it fails, death occurs quickly, and until fairly recently little could be done for a person with a failing heart.

In the early 1900s, the idea of replacing an unhealthy organ with a healthy one from a donor moved from the realm of science fiction to that of scientific possibility. This type of process first appeared in the world of agriculture. Even thousands of years ago, primitive farmers knew that one could dig up a live plant, bury it in another location, and the plant would continue to live. This was called transplantation. Both ancient Egyptian warriors and Italian doctors in the Middle Ages experimented with skin grafting, a method of transplanting healthy skin onto a wounded area. This was only successful when the donor and recipient were the same person.

While the idea of transplanting organs has been widely described in mythology and literature, Mary Shelley's 1818 novel *Frankenstein* is perhaps the best known example. The story of Dr. Frankenstein, a doctor who creates a creature from the "donated" body parts of corpses, is one of the most famous novels of the nineteenth century.

In real life, transplanting dead organs is impossible because of disease and decay. But beginning about a century ago, scientists began experimenting with live organ transplant.

In 1905, Alexis Carrel and Charles Guthrie developed a new technique to connect blood vessels. They applied their technique to transplantation, transplanting a healthy heart from one dog onto the neck of another (the recipient retained its own heart). Although the dog died from a blood clot less than two hours later, the experiment was considered successful.

In 1954, the first kidney transplant was performed; in 1963, the first liver transplant. Transplanting a heart would seem to be the next logical step. The problem was, until the 1960s, patients were not declared dead until their heart had stopped beating. By the time this happened, the heart was usually unsuitable for donation. Only by declaring a patient "brain dead" or lacking brain function—even if the

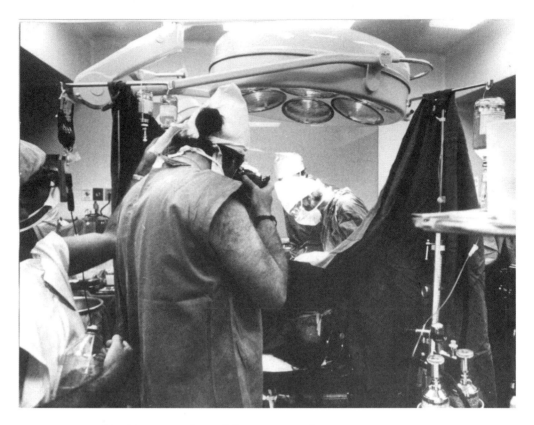

Dr. Barnard and his team during surgery

heart was still beating—could a heart be harvested, or removed from the chest of the patient, and transplanted.

While many doctors knew how to perform a heart transplant, their unwillingness to take the risk of declaring a patient brain dead prevented them from performing the operation.

There was one exception.

The surgeon who performed the world's first human heart transplant was born into rural poverty. He would grow up to become one of the most famous surgeons the world has ever known. He would be a millionaire many times over and would date famous actresses and models.

Yet he didn't gain recognition for inventing a new surgical technique or discovering a cure. When he performed the world's first heart transplant, the operation had already been mapped out by others, every step carefully detailed.

Dr. Hillel Laks explained that what this man did was own the courage to risk both failure and professional criticism. "He reasoned that if people are clearly going to die, you were justified in starting a [transplant] trial even when you don't have all the answers," Dr. Laks told the *Los Angeles Times*. "Because he started, other investigators were spurred to find answers to the problems."

The first heart transplant was an enormous risk, but since that first operation, more than 100,000 similar surgeries have been performed worldwide. In the United States, an estimated 2,400 patients receive transplanted hearts every year. Eighty-seven percent of them survive for over a year, and nearly 75 percent are still alive five years later. They owe those years of extra life to the courage of one surgeon.

His name was Christiaan Barnard. This is his story.

At one time in his life, Christiaan Barnard would have given anything to be seen with a pretty woman. After he became famous, he reached celebrity status. Dr. Barnard found that he could have his choice of women. In 1969, his first wife Aletta and he divorced. In 1970, Dr. Barnard married 19-year-old Barbara Zoellner, shown here.

Chapter 2
A Rural Childhood

I nside the South African church, parishioners listened as Maria Elisabeth Barnard played the organ. To most of the congregation, the instrument's music was a soulful interlude, but to young Christiaan it was something more. When the child pumped the organ's bellows, he considered the action of the instrument. As he recalled in *Time* magazine, "Maybe that's where, subconsciously, I started getting interested in the pump, which is all the heart is after all."

Christiaan Neethling Barnard was born on November 8, 1922, in Beaufort West, South Africa, a landscape far different from the ones he'd enjoy in later years. Located in the Cape Province section of the country, 250 miles north of Cape Town, it was a dirty, dusty, sun-bleached region, filled with poverty and disease. In many respects this region of South Africa, known as the Karoo, resembles Arizona, but the lives of the region's inhabitants are far different from those of Arizona's.

Despite its seemingly barren landscape, the Karoo's scrubs support flocks of sheep. The animals are utilized entirely, from the wool for clothing to the mutton from their flanks for food. The majority of the residents are quite poor, surviving on income from their animals and subsistence farming.

Christiaan's father, Adam Hendrik, was an educated man, but his choice of profession guaranteed the family's lifestyle would be as impoverished as the locals'.

Adam Hendrik began his working life as an unsuccessful salesman, and then as an officer in the Salvation Army. Before Christiaan was born, Adam began working as a Dutch Reformed missionary, a Calvinist. Inspired by the messages of John Calvin, a sixteenth-century Protestant theologian, Calvinism holds that salvation can be obtained only through God's grace. It is a religion that emphasizes hard work, simplicity, and sacrifice. All of those elements were present in the Barnard household.

While Adam preached the word of God, he emphasized the importance of racial tolerance.

The country in which Christiaan was raised, South Africa, was colonized by the Dutch and the English in the 1600s. Although their power struggles and fighting over land led to the establishment of separate territories, the English, following the discovery of diamonds around 1900, invaded Dutch-run land. The Boer War that resulted led to eventual independence from England. After a series of power shifts, the Afrikaner National Party began dominating South African life in the 1940s.

It was this party that pushed forward the principle of apartheid, or "apartness." The goal of apartheid was to maintain racial separation and ensure white domination.

Apartheid laws were passed in 1948. Every aspect of life, from land ownership to the prohibition of interracial marriages, was impacted by these laws. Everyone was racially classified: white, black or African, or colored (mixed race, including many Indians and Asians). As a result of these laws, whites, who comprised less than 25 percent of the population, owned 87 percent of the land and had 75 percent of the national income.

Even prior to these laws, when Christiaan was still a young boy, racial segregation and laws favoring whites were already in place. As an example, every night at nine o'clock, a boy would ring a bell in Beaufort West. The clang was a signal. It meant that everyone who wasn't white had to leave and go to their own homes. Being caught in town after nine o'clock, unless one was white, was a criminal offense.

Adam Barnard's congregation was made up almost exclusively of the so-called colored, or racially mixed, people; because of this the family was shunned by their neighbors, who were mainly poor whites. Christiaan's father was a pioneer, similar in some respects to the many white Americans who became involved in the U.S. civil rights movement in the 1950s and '60s. Adam Barnard didn't march or protest. He just practiced what he preached.

"Son," he once told young Christiaan, "for some people the mills of God grind slowly but surely." In other words, eventually justice would come for his congregation, as well as to the rest of the oppressed peoples of South Africa.

As a missionary, Adam's wages were quite low. During his career he never earned more than $750 a year. Even in the 1930s, this wasn't much. Often Christiaan and his four brothers subsisted on fruits, vegetables, and walnuts fresh from the family garden. Other times the family survived just on bread and the lard from fried sheep's tails. Sometimes there wasn't enough money for new clothes or even shoes.

"We were poor. We never had shoes," Christiaan recalled in the book *The Transplanted Heart* by Peter Hawthorne. "Even in winter we walked barefoot. I remember coming home with painful cracks in my feet from the cold. I used to soak them in a mixture of candle wax and paraffin to take out the sting."

This lack didn't deter young Christiaan. He once won a mile race running barefoot.

At night, like a young Abe Lincoln, Christiaan conducted his studies by firelight. Among his many chores at the family's modest home, with its corrugated iron roof, was gathering firewood so that the Barnards could heat their home, cook their food, and boil their water. For extra money, Christiaan worked as a caddy at a local golf course.

It was a difficult childhood. But looking back, Christiaan Barnard saw the advantages in it. "That part of my life influenced me tremendously," he once said in an interview. "It taught me to persevere, to have a goal and to reach it."

He was also encouraged by his mother, Maria Elisabeth. In an age when most women with families stayed home, Maria worked full-time. She passed on her strong work ethic to her offspring and demanded that all her sons rank first in their class. Of all her boys, Christiaan, with his regularly high marks and scholarship, gained her favor the most.

"My mother taught me ambition . . . ," Christiaan admitted to *Time* magazine; "but she also tempered it with humility. I think that helped me later in life. Whatever happened to me, I always tended to find time for everybody."

In the Barnard household, even more difficult than poverty were the deaths of several Barnard children. Two of them died in infancy. In some respects, young Christiaan was a "miracle baby"—a child not expected, whom his parents pampered as best they could. Another child died when Christiaan was about four.

"I don't remember him," Christiaan told *Time* magazine, "but my father once showed me a little biscuit with the boy's teeth marks in it. Now I look back and I see pictures of the little boy and the terrible suffering in his face, and I realize that he died of a heart problem and that had he lived in my time, I, as a cardiac surgeon, probably could have cured him."

The deaths impacted his family and influenced the way his parents cared for their surviving children. While most parents treat their children as special, Christiaan's mother and father became even more involved in their kids' lives.

Education was very important, even if there was little money. Christiaan's parents wanted all of their boys to go to college. Getting a good education meant more than just a chance to earn a decent living: It meant having the opportunity to make a difference in people's lives. In the end Johannes (nicknamed Barney) and Marius would both graduate from college. Christiaan's older brother, Dodsley, was the first to attend a school of higher education, majoring in mechanical engineering.

Christiaan looked up to Dodsley and believed he too would someday study mechanical engineering. That changed when Christiaan was a young teen and Dodsley returned home in disgrace. He'd failed two years of studies and "the house was in mourning," Christiaan once said, describing the resulting mood in the Barnard household.

After Dodsley's arrival home, he took Christiaan aside and told him he should consider becoming a doctor. Christiaan's other older brother, Barney, agreed. "He had quite a few medical students as friends and they would all kid me that I was the one in the family who should become a doctor," Christiaan admitted in *The Transplanted Heart*. "They said there was money in medicine, it was a lucrative profession and they told me about people becoming rich in private practice."

Perhaps being motivated by money wasn't terribly noble. But then again, considering the dire poverty of his surroundings, young Christiaan's desire for wealth was hardly surprising. Besides, Christiaan was convinced he could help people, as his father had hoped, while still becoming successful.

Young Christiaan had diversions beyond his studies. He was an active tennis player, once winning a championship despite his use of a borrowed racket and the need to stuff his sneakers with strips of cardboard to cover the holes.

And he discovered girls.

"To me at fourteen, love was to hold a girl's hand, wind up the gramophone," he said in an interview with *People Weekly*. "To dance with a girl, oh my God!"

At eighteen, Christiaan Barnard left his rural home for the big city of Cape Town. He was embarking on the journey that would eventually fulfill all his dreams—to have wealth, to help people, and, of course, to win the admiration of women.

Princess Grace of Monaco has dinner with Christiaan Barnard in Monte Carlo, Monaco on August 9, 1968.

Dr. Barnard is shown here with his first wife Aletta and their two children, Dierdre then 17 and Andre then 16. His son Andre later followed his father into the medical field.

Chapter Three
Some Lucky Failings

● ●

Walking five miles through the streets of Cape Town, beneath the blanketing rain gusting off Table Mountain, Christiaan Barnard made his daily journey from the tiny apartment he shared with his brother Barney to the university. There may have been more scholarly or talented students than Christiaan, but there was probably none as dedicated.

"I had no money to buy myself a raincoat," he recalled in *The Transplanted Heart.* "I remember how I used to sit in the bus shelters shivering in wet clothes, waiting for it to stop pouring."

The University of Cape Town (UCT) attracted the children of some of South Africa's most prominent citizens. Founded in 1829 as South African College, and originally a school for boys, by the late 1800s and early 1900s the government had funded its establishment as a university. Founded in 1918, UCT would soon gain a reputation as a top-notch research facility.

By the time of Christiaan's attendance, the school boasted a well-funded medical school and a teaching hospital, all located on the scenic grounds of the Groote Schuur Campus, a donated estate resting in the shadows of the famous Devil's Peak.

Although Christiaan was ranked only in the middle of his class, he was also burdened by greater financial obstacles than most of his peers. Unsupported by his parents,

Christiaan worked a series of odd jobs to make ends meet. When he graduated with dual bachelor degrees in medicine and surgery, he began working as an intern at Groote Schuur Hospital, and although the salary was quite low, there *was* a salary. He even had enough money to take his new girlfriend, nurse Aletta Louw, out to the occasional movie.

After a year, Christiaan made a decision his father would be proud of—one that wouldn't make him wealthy but would definitely help others. Christiaan couldn't forget his roots. He'd spent his childhood surrounded by the poverty of the parishioners at his father's church and of other neighbors. As he grew older, he deeply understood the unique medical challenges faced by those with little access to money or medical care. So instead of following the path set by many of his peers and accepting a job at a posh medical center, he joined two other doctors in a general practice at Ceres, a small farming village 100 miles north of Cape Town.

Choosing to become a general practitioner meant he would treat a variety of medical conditions, from minor illnesses to the types of crippling injuries suffered on farm equipment. Quite a few of the patients he encountered had never been to a doctor before. Some couldn't pay for their treatment. Barnard helped them all.

Because of the three doctors' willingness to help everyone, the business lost money, and just two years after joining the practice, Christiaan was asked to leave. Although he loved the job and was sad when he lost it, he began to consider other options.

During his two years in general practice, Christiaan was most affected by the children he encountered. Sometimes malnourished, they often suffered from diseases that rarely affected the middle class. The most heartbreaking were the tiniest victims, infants who'd suffered from birth defects, due in part to their mother's diet and lifestyle during pregnancy.

Touched by their plight, Christiaan began work as a senior medical resident at the City Hospital in Cape Town, which served a poor area comprised mainly of people of mixed racial heritage. He began studying the treatment of birth defects and illnesses such as tubercular meningitis, because, as he recalled in *The Transplanted Heart*, "the treatment at that time was poor and I tried to find new methods." It was during this period that he first became truly interested in the research aspects of medicine, a passion that would inspire him to conduct a series of experiments.

Socially, Barnard's life was moving forward as well. He and Aletta married in 1948. Aletta, a former nurse, was prepared to help out with expenses while Christiaan continued to pursue his dreams as a doctor.

During his years of training, Barnard's family grew. By 1953 it included two children: a daughter, Deirdre, and a son, Andre.

In 1953 he completed his doctoral thesis, called "The Treatment of Tubercular Meningitis," and was awarded his M.D. (doctor of medicine degree) "on the grounds of research studies of outstanding quality."

But Christiaan—now Dr. Barnard—wanted more. He wanted to become a surgeon.

To many, surgery is considered the highest level of medicine a doctor can achieve. It requires extensive medical knowledge, skillful hand-eye coordination, and dexterity. Dr. Barnard believed he possessed these qualities. He began specializing in surgery at Groote Schuur Hospital, where his superiors were impressed with the obvious talents he displayed. Still, he quickly realized the greatest advances in surgerical techniques were occurring in Western Europe and the United States. However, travel to these schools was expensive, and he knew he couldn't afford it on his own. He applied for a bursary—a scholarship—at several medical schools in England. He was rejected.

His rejection turned out to be one of those "lucky failures" that mark the lives of many successful people. "I've had a lot of lucky choices forced on me in my life," Barnard admitted to *Time* magazine. One of those, he said, was "applying for a bursary in England and being turned down. If I'd got it, I would never have become a heart surgeon because they weren't that far advanced in heart surgery."

Then he got the opportunity he'd been waiting for. "I was approached one day, quite out of the blue, by old Professor Brock, chief lecturer in medicine at the University of Cape Town," he recounted in *The Transplanted Heart.* "He asked me if I would like to work in the United States—just like that. I didn't hesitate. 'Yes,' I said. But I still had to consult my wife."

His wife didn't hesitate, either. Although their relative poverty meant he would have to go to the United States first, then see if he could earn enough to send for his family, the couple realized it would be the best preparation for their future.

In 1955, Dr. Christiaan Barnard left for the University of Minnesota to begin training with some of the most innovative heart surgeons in the world.

Training at the University of Minnesota, Dr. Barnard was able to study under some of the best-known heart specialists in the world, including Dr. Owen Wangensteen, shown here.

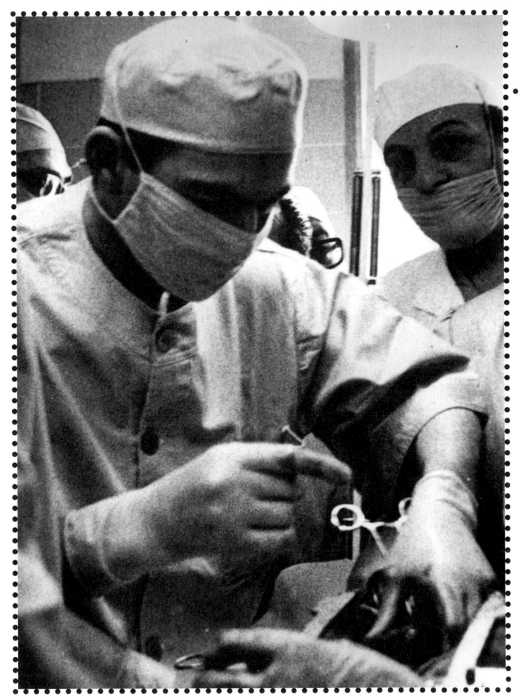

Dr. Barnard began his experiments with heart transplants on dogs. Here he operates on a dog at La Paz Hospital in Madrid, Spain.

Chapter Four

Getting to the Heart of It

• •

As a teenager, surrounded by poverty while dreaming of training to be a doctor, Christiaan Barnard was different. Attending university alongside the children of the wealthy, Christiaan Barnard, the offspring of an itinerant missionary, was different. And while studying to become a heart surgeon, Christiaan Barnard was different.

Dr. Barnard's South African medical degree left him unqualified to practice medicine in the United States. Even if he had been qualified, with all his advanced studies there was little time to earn money as a doctor. Instead this well-educated physician turned to the types of odd jobs he'd done as an adolescent, mowing lawns for five dollars apiece and washing cars.

Despite having to work at manual labor in his spare time, and being separated from his wife and young children, who'd remained behind in South Africa, Dr. Barnard considered the sacrifices worth it. Attending the University of Minnesota, he was able to study under some of the best-known heart specialists in the world, people like Drs. Richard Varco, Owen H. Wangensteen, and C. Walton Lillehei. By far the greatest influence of all the people he studied under came from the pair of doctors who would later perfect heart transplant techniques. Drs. Norman Schumway and Richard R. Lower provided Barnard with a valuable understanding of the latest in heart surgery techniques. In 1959, a few years after Dr. Barnard left the United States, the pair would perform the first successful heart transplant on a dog. The animal survived for eight days. Eventually, by perfecting the technique, they would increase the survival expectancy to eighteen months.

The technique they taught, which would later be applied by Dr. Barnard, was well described in the book *Heart Transplant* by Marais Malan: "One of the main elements in Dr. Schumway's successful technique, which differentiates it from other suggested heart transplant methods, is that it does not require removal of the entire heart. He leaves part of the walls of the upper part of the heart, containing the veins, in the recipient when removing the sick heart. This makes the operation easier because only the heart tissues and arteries have to be sewn when the new heart is implanted."

Under the tutelage of these well-known heart experts, Dr. Barnard began to assist in a variety of complicated procedures. In the middle 1950s, open-heart surgery was a growing field, in part because of the new technologies that were being utilized, such as the heart-lung machine. Developed in 1955, this innovation was a mechanical pump that maintained circulation of the blood during heart surgery by taking blood away from the heart, oxygenating it, and then returning it to the body. It made such invasive procedures as open-heart surgery much safer, although certainly not risk-free.

Dr. Barnard began to work on his own innovations, including most notably an aortic valve prosthesis that could be substituted for the aorta. He also came up with a new technique for treating congenital (or existing from birth) lesions and a heart disease known as Ebstein's anomaly.

He wrote papers on everything from the aortic valve to the process of testing and designing the aortic valve prosthesis. The work he did at the University of Minnesota was part of the reason he would claim in interviews that the two years he spent in the United States made up the most fascinating time of his life.

His life was not free from struggle, however. Money was always a problem. After he received a much-needed $2,000 award, he was able to send for his wife and two small children. Still, the money was quickly consumed by the family, and Dr. Barnard, a future heart surgeon, continued to support them by selling newspapers and working as a private nurse. Despite his efforts, the family ran out of money and, sadly, his wife and children returned to South Africa.

Dr. Barnard missed both his family and his homeland deeply, but he knew there was still much to learn. He honed his skills with studies at the University of Virginia before returning to Minnesota, where his dedication and focus soon became legendary. Once, in order to solve an issue involving intestinal abnormalities in newborns, he operated on forty-nine dogs before solving the problem on his fiftieth attempt.

"That was typical of his singleness of purpose," Dr. Owen H. Wangensteen, a research surgeon and one of his teachers at the school, recalled in *The Transplanted Heart.* "He was the sort of person you didn't have to drive. He drove himself hard enough."

When his studies ended, university officials asked him if there was something he'd like to bring back to South Africa. The answer was easy: money.

He wanted to get Groote Schuur its own heart-lung machine, a piece of equipment worth several thousand dollars. Not only did the University of Minnesota agree to fund this, they promised Dr. Barnard several thousand dollars more a year in grant money. The reply to the request taught him a valuable lesson—to never be afraid to ask for money for his dreams. In 1957, Dr. Barnard returned to his homeland, planning on perfecting an open-heart surgery procedure. Instead, in less than a decade, he would accomplish more than he could ever imagine.

Dr. Barnard addressed a group of journalists in Redenbosch Cape Town, South Africa, in December 1967. He explained how he performed a heart transplant at Groote Schuur Hospital on December 2, 1967.

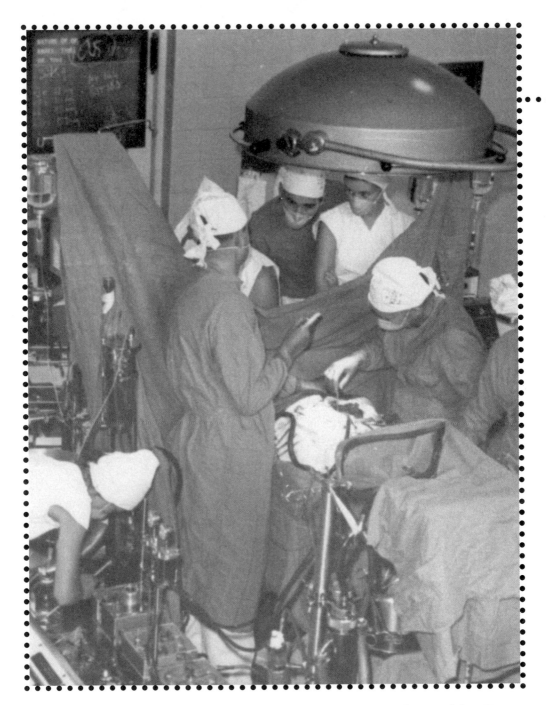

This is the scene of open heart surgery being performed by Dr. Christiaan Barnard's team at Groote Schuur Hospital in Cape Town, South Africa.

Chapter Five
The Operation

• •

Arriving at Groote Schuur Hospital, not far from where he'd gone to college, Dr. Christiaan Barnard was a man possessed. He'd worked hard in the United States for two years, surviving poverty and hardship, all to perfect his abilities as a heart surgeon. He not only had the skills, he had the equipment, having purchased a heart-lung machine for the hospital with the grant from the University of Minnesota.

Yet one of the most crucial procedures—open-heart surgery—was not being performed at the hospital. Even worse, administrators were reluctant to approve what many still considered experimental surgery. Dr. Barnard refused to give up. Eventually the operation was approved.

In 1957, Dr. Barnard performed the first open-heart surgery at Groote Schuur Hospital. "I was so worked up over it," he recalled in *The Transplanted Heart*. I never slept the night before. I kept on going through the different moves and procedures in my mind. I was terribly nervous. We operated on a twelve-year-old Colored [mixed race] child. A simple operation without complications."

At least not for the patient. For the doctor it was a different story. During the procedure Dr. Barnard became aware of an unfamiliar stiffness and pain in his fingers. At first he believed it was simply related to the intensity of the surgery. Eventually, however, Barnard realized he had to see a doctor.

Barnard found out he had arthritis, a painful inflammation of the joints. For many people arthritis is a

33, 367

natural part of growing older; for a young surgeon at the beginning of his career, the diagnosis was heartbreaking. Eventually his hands wouldn't be able to perform operations. The only good news was that the day when he'd be unable to operate was in the distant future.

Barnard did not allow himself time for self-pity. Instead, he embarked on another quest, one far more challenging than convincing his superiors at the hospital to allow him to perform open-heart surgery. Dr. Christiaan Barnard wanted to perform a heart transplant operation.

The operation, which involves replacing a sick and dying heart with a fresh and healthy one, taken from another person who is dying, couldn't be more dramatic. Already livers and kidneys had been successfully transplanted, and to Dr. Barnard the heart wasn't a source of mystery. There was nothing poetic about it—it was a pump, nothing more. While the operation was challenging, already his old mentor Dr. Schumway was performing the transplant on dogs.

In order to fulfill this dream, Barnard began to assemble a team at the J. S. Marais Research Laboratory, a square building with the rounded, skylit roof of an observatory, not far from the University of Cape Town's department of surgery. Among the team of surgeons and lab assistants was Christiaan Barnard's brother, Marius, himself a gifted surgeon. Marius Barnard would play an important part in the progress toward a successful heart transplant operation, overseeing much of the research and assisting his brother during experimental operations, which were conducted primarily on dogs and baboons, which were plentiful in South Africa.

They initially began working with the aortic valves, part of the body's main artery. They crafted artificial substitutes for the dogs, put the dogs on the heart-lung machine, and performed endless series of open-heart surgeries, hoping both to increase their knowledge and to prepare for the unexpected. Throughout the ten years they worked, there was never much money; but then the Barnards, more than their colleagues, were used to getting by on less. Whenever they couldn't afford to buy a piece of equipment, they just figured out a way to make it themselves.

In early 1965, they attempted their first heart transplant on a dog. Although Marius would describe the operation by saying, "It wasn't too bad," the dog died—as did the next forty-nine on which they operated.

"Some people call it failing," Marius admitted in *The Transplanted Heart.* "We weren't successful, that's true, but we didn't fail. We weren't so very keen on long-term results to study because we thought, Schumway and these people have done it already and it's a lot of extra organization and a lot more work. Most of these dogs we could keep alive for eighteen hours. Which was all we needed."

Although the deaths of so many experimental animals were indeed a tragedy, the people involved believed they were a necessary part of the process.

In 1967, the surgical team was put on alert. Given the right set of conditions, they believed they were ready to perform the first heart transplant. So, too, were a number of other surgical teams across the globe, including Dr. Schumway's.

In preparation, Dr. Christiaan Barnard performed a number of kidney transplants. And for the first, but not the last time, he found himself in a swirling hurricane of controversy. In several cases he implanted the donor kidneys of an African (or black) person into a white South African. While not technically forbidden under the nation's apartheid laws, it was definitely controversial. Dr. Barnard found such discussions ridiculous. A kidney was a kidney, a heart was a heart, and to him there were only two types: healthy or sick. Color just didn't matter.

A less successful but equally controversial operation was one called xeno-transplantation. First tried by James Hardy at the University of Mississippi in 1964, it involves transplanting the organ of an animal—usually a primate—into a human patient. Dr. Hardy transplanted a chimp heart into a sixty-eight-year-old man. In 1967, Dr. Barnard performed the same procedure, twice: once on a twenty-five-year-old woman, who received a baboon heart, and then again on a sixty-year-old man, who got a chimp heart. Both of these patients died very quickly.

Despite the number of teams across the country, including Dr. Norman Schumway's and Dr. Richard R. Lower's, and the fact that the techniques taught by Schumway were considered applicable to human patients, many surgeons were reluctant even to attempt the procedure. They hesitated because with other organ transplants, the donor was considered dead when the heart stopped beating. Unfortunately, waiting for a heart to stop would often leave it unsuitable for harvesting. In order for a donor heart to be taken, in most cases the doctors couldn't wait for the heart to stop beating but instead had to rely on measuring brain activity. If there was no brain activity, the patient could be declared "brain dead" and life support would be "unplugged." This is standard procedure now, but in the late 1960s it wasn't just controversial, it was potentially illegal. Indeed, Schumway and Lower were later tried for murder when they removed the life-support equipment from a potential donor. Although they were found not guilty, in 1967, unplugging life support was a risky move.

Dr. Christiaan Barnard wasn't afraid of risks. All his team needed was an appropriate donor.

On December 2, 1967, in a Cape Town festive with preparations for the upcoming holidays, the Darvall family went out for a drive in daughter Denise's brand-new car. Denise, twenty-five, was a quiet and conservative bank teller who had never been married or had a serious boyfriend. Her work at the bank and her family were her whole life. On that fateful Saturday, Denise was enjoying showing off her new car.

The accident didn't happen in the vehicle.

Denise parked and got out with her mother, Myrtle Ann. The two headed to a local bakery. They purchased a caramel cake and left, crossing Main Street. They never saw the approaching car.

Both Denise and Myrtle Ann were hit. Myrtle Ann died instantly.

Denise was critically injured but clinging to life. Her brain was irreparably damaged by the blow.

Passing the accident, pausing as she drove around the wreckage, was Ann Washkansky, the wife of a dying grocer.

She did not know the ways the tragedy would soon touch her life.

Less than a mile away, Ann's husband, Louis Washkansky, was in Groote Schuur Hospital, his home for the previous three months. His heart was failing, and he was near death.

Denise Darvall and Louis Washkansky were about to be inextricably linked in history.

The grocer had made his decision on November 10: He had nothing to lose and decided to risk the transplant operation.

The other decision was Edward Darvall's. He was Denise's father.

It was after midnight at Groote Schuur when a pair of surgeons approached Edward Darvall. There would be no more bad news. He'd already learned his daughter was dying. The two men offered him hope. In a small way his daughter could live on—with her organs in the bodies of others.

Edward Darvall was told of the grocer's fate, and that Denise showed no brain activity. He was asked if he would consider allowing his daughter's heart to be donated to the dying man. According to those present, Darvall took a breath and then quietly, sadly, replied, "If there is no hope for my daughter, then you must try to save this man."

In an interview with *The New York Times*, Christiaan Barnard vividly described what happened next:

"As soon as the donor died, we opened her chest and connected her to a heart-lung machine, suffusing [spreading through with liquid] her body so we could keep the heart alive. I cut out the heart. We examined it, and as soon as we found it was normal, we put it in a dish containing solution at 10 degrees centigrade to cool it down further.

"We then transferred this heart to the operating room where we had the patient and we connected it to the heart-lung machine. From the time we cut out the heart it was four minutes until we had oxygenated blood going back to the heart muscle from the donor's heart-lung machine. We then excised the patient's heart.

"The donor heart was sutured in place, the organ was warmed gently and as it approached normal body temperature it started to beat vigorously."

The operation was a success.

"The heart transplant wasn't such a big thing surgically," Dr. Barnard admitted in *Time* magazine. "The technique was a basic one. The point is that I was prepared to take a risk."

Dr. Marius Barnard, along with other members of the surgical team, attended Denise Darvall's funeral. After observing a few minutes of silence, Marius, his voice choked with emotion, told those assembled, "Just think, will you. That girl is being cremated today. And her heart is still alive."

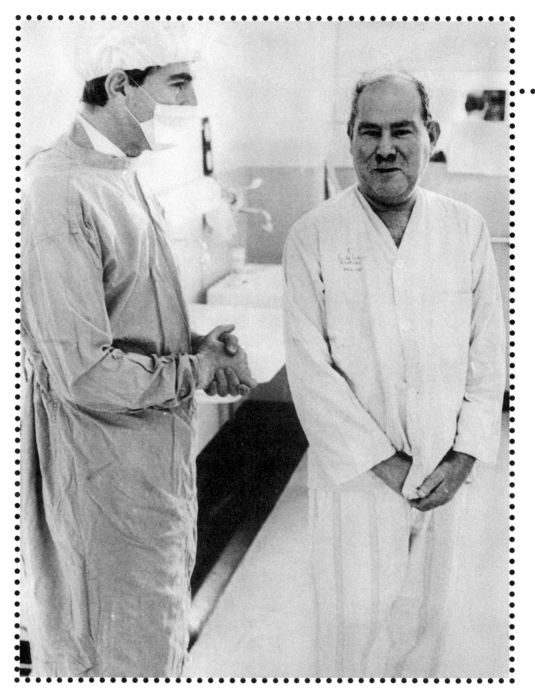

In 1968, Dr. Barnard gave dentist Philip Blaiberg a new heart. Barnard (left) is shown in this photo with Blaiberg at Groote Schuur Hospital.

Chapter Six

Fame!

● ●

The heart transplant operation performed by Dr. Christiaan Barnard was considered a success, but it did little for Louis Washkansky. It offered the dying grocer only eighteen more days of life. Vulnerable to infection because of the massive doses of immune-suppressing drugs he needed to take in order to force his body to accept the donated heart, he died from pneumonia.

Despite the outcome, the news of the heart transplant spanned the globe, offering a glimmer of hope to the thousands of people risking heart failure.

It didn't just alter the lives of potential recipients. It also changed the life of Dr. Barnard forever. He was young for a surgeon, and good-looking. His picture was plastered across newspapers in practically every country in the world; he was interviewed on radio and television. In a very short time he became perhaps the most famous surgeon the world has ever known.

The notoriety would overshadow all his later accomplishments.

He continued to perform the operation for the next three years, with similar results. Across the world, other surgeons, including Dr. Schumway, emboldened by Dr. Barnard, also performed the operation.

Unable to increase the survival rate of his patients, Dr. Barnard experimented with a new technique. Called heterotopic heart transplant, it involved leaving much of the original heart in place and attaching a donor heart. The original heart became a sort of backup system. This unusual technique was more successful, with 50 percent of the patients surviving for one year, and some living over a decade.

While his professional career was successful following the first transplant, his personal life grew more turbulent. He became involved with a series of actresses, including Sophia Loren and Gina Lollobrigida, two famous Italian movie stars. In 1969, Aletta divorced him. The next year he married Barbara Zoellner, who was eighteen when they met and the daughter of a wealthy and prominent family in South Africa. The couple would have two children, Frederick and Christiaan, Jr., before divorcing in 1982.

Besides just the marriages, other aspects of his life were changing. "[T]he operation, and its significance as the first of its kind, took me into another world—not just professionally but personally and socially as well. I loved it," he confided to *Time* magazine. "I love people, I love the female sex, and I like to enjoy life. I'm easy to party with."

Throughout the rest of his life, Dr. Barnard would become a regular fixture on the international party circuit, enjoying dinners and drinks with some of the most prominent people in the world. His life knew tragedy as well, particularly in 1984 when his son Andre, by then a doctor himself, died from an apparent drug overdose. His death was labeled a suicide.

"A friend of mine pointed out that 70 percent of people who commit or attempt to commit suicide come from a broken home," Dr. Barnard told the BBC. Choking back tears, he continued, "I think I should have done more. I was so busy, running around so much, that I neglected my son. I believe if I paid more attention, maybe he would not have committed suicide."

Professionally, Dr. Barnard continued to run several research labs, but he also retired from his job at the hospital in 1983 when the arthritis that had plagued him for over twenty years finally meant he'd no longer be able to perform surgery. He advised a heart transplant program in Oklahoma City and took a position as scientist in residence at Baptist Medical Center in 1984. By then, improved antirejection drugs such as cyclosporine had reduced the difficulties involved with heart transplants—the only issue being a lack of suitable donors for the many patients who needed them.

In the middle 1980s, Glycel, a line of $200-a-bottle skin cream touted as an antiaging formula, was introduced to the world. Dr. Barnard, himself so terrified of appearing old that he sought out a variety of expensive treatments, endorsed the product for a reported payment of $4 million. His professional reputation was forever tarnished when, following an investigation by the Food and Drug Administration, the product was pulled from the shelves the next year.

After his marriage to Barbara Zoellner dissolved, he quickly remarried, wedding former model Karin Setzkorn when she was still in her twenties. The couple would have two children before divorcing in 1999.

In an interview with Rediff on the Net, Dr. Barnard promised, "When I die I can say, 'Thank you, God. I have had a great opportunity in life.'"

On September 2, 2001, following an early-morning swim at the coastal resort of Paphos in Cyprus, Dr. Christiaan Barnard suffered a fatal asthma attack. Soon after, in an interview with *People Weekly,* his daughter Deirdre said of her father, "He could stand to be alone, but he could not stand loneliness. The man belonged to the world."

Chronology

1922—Christiaan Neethling Barnard is born in Beaufort West, South Africa, on November 8.

1946—Receives bachelor's degrees in medicine and surgery from University of Cape Town; interns at Groote Schuur Hospital.

1947—Works as a general practitioner in Ceres, South Africa.

1948—Marries Aletta Louw, a nurse; researches birth defects at the City Hospital in Cape Town.

1952—Daughter Deirdre is born.

1953—Son Andre is born; receives M.D. from University of Cape Town.

1955—Enrolls at University of Minnesota at Minneapolis, studying general surgery.

1957—During first open-heart surgery at Groote Schuur Hospital, becomes aware of arthritis.

1958—Forms research team at the J. S. Marais Research Laboratory at University of Cape Town.

1967—Performs first heart transplant between humans.

1969—Divorces Aletta Louw.

1970—Marries nineteen-year-old Johannesburg socialite Barbara Zoellner.

1972—Son Frederick is born.

1974—Son Christiaan, Jr., is born.

1982—Divorces Barbara Zoellner.

1983—Retires from surgery due to crippling arthritis.

1984—Becomes scientist in residence at Baptist Medical Center in Oklahoma City; son Andre dies of a drug overdose.

1988—Marries model Karin Setzkorn.

1999—Divorces Karin Setzkorn.

2001—Dies from fatal asthma attack on September 2.

Time Line of Discovery

14th Century—Italian surgeons graft skin from patient's arm onto injuries to heal wounds.

1628—English physician William Harvey discovers the circulation of the blood.

1812—Julian Jean Cesar La Gallois suggests that a continuing injection of blood could keep alive someone whose heart has failed.

1880—Henry Martin builds a "heart-lung preparation," a machine designed to pump blood through the organs.

1905—Alexis Carrel and Charles Guthrie successfully transplant a heart from one dog to another dog's neck.

1928—E. H. J. Schuster and H. H. Dale announce the construction of a pump to circulate blood through an animal without using the animal's heart.

1930s—Transatlantic pilot Charles Lindbergh and Alexis Carrel market their Lindbergh pump.

1952—General Motors researcher F. D. Dodrill uses a mechanical heart to keep a patient alive for nearly an hour during surgery.

1952—Charles Hufnagel develops a plastic aortic valve.

1954— Joseph E. Murray transplants a kidney between identical twins at Brigham & Women's Hospital in Boston.

1955—C. Walton Lillehei and Richard DeWall invent the bubble oxygenator, which, when used with a pump, acts as a heart-lung machine.

1959—Norman Schumway and Richard R. Lower perform the first successful heart transplant from one dog to the chest of another dog.

1964—James Hardy at the University of Mississippi transplants a chimp heart into a 68-year-old man.

1966—Richard Lillehei at the University of Minnesota transplants a pancreas, kidney, and part of the small intestines.

1967—Christiaan Barnard performs xeno-transplantation on a twenty-five-year-old woman, who receives a baboon heart, and a sixty-year-old-man, who gets a chimp heart; in December, Barnard performs first heart transplant between humans.

Glossary

aorta—The body's main artery, it carries oxygenated blood from the heart's left ventricle to the entire body except the lungs.

artery—Any of the thick blood vessels that carry blood through the body from the heart.

artificial heart—A mechanical device designed as a replacement (either temporarily or permanently) for a nonfunctioning heart.

atrium—One of the two upper chambers (or atria) of the heart, its primary purpose is to receive blood from the veins.

capillaries—The body's tiniest blood vessels, they transport blood from the arteries to the tissues of the body and are drained by the veins.

cardiac—Related to the heart.

cardiac arrest—The cessation, or stopping, of the heartbeat and cardiac function, ending circulation of the blood and often resulting in death.

cardiovascular—Related to the heart and blood vessels.

donor—A patient who provides organs for transplant.

harvesting—Removal of organs from a patient's body to be used in a transplant procedure.

heart-lung machine—A device designed to take over the work of the heart during open-heart surgery, adding oxygen to the blood before the blood is returned to the body.

recipient—A patient who receives a donated organ.

transplant—The replacement of a damaged organ with a healthy one.

valve—A structure found in blood vessels that allows the flow of blood in one direction only.

vein—Blood vessels that carry blood to the heart from the rest of the body.

ventricle—One of the two lower chambers in the heart. The right ventricle pumps blood to the lungs; the left ventricle pumps the newly oxygenated blood through the rest of the body.

Further Reading

Books

Fox, Renée C., and Judith P. Swazey. *Spare Parts: Organ Replacement in American Society.* New York: Oxford Press, 1992.

Hawthorne, Peter. *The Transplanted Heart.* New York: Rand McNally and Company, 1970.

Malan, Marais. *Heart Transplant: The Story of Barnard and the Ultimate in Cardiac Surgery.* Johannesburg, South Africa: Voortrekkerpers, Ltd., 1968.

Simon, Seymour. *The Heart: Our Circulation System.* New York: Morrow Junior Books, 1996.

Periodicals

Altman, Lawrence K. "Christiaan Barnard, 78, Surgeon for First Heart Transplant, Dies." *New York Times,* September 3, 2001, p. A-1.

Clark, Matt, et al. "An Incredible Affair of the Heart." *Newsweek,* December 13, 1982, p. 70.

Cooper, David K. C. "Profiles in Cardiology: Christiaan Neethling Barnard." *Clinical Cardiology,* July 2001.

Dougherty, Steven, and Drusilla Menaker. "Lion in Winter; Christiaan Barnard has had fame, scandal—and few regrets." *People Weekly,* April 8, 1996, v. 45, p. 117.

Hawthorne, Peter (as told to). "Heart to Heart." *Time,* September 3, 2001, v. 158, i. 9, p. G6.

"Health: Christiaan Barnard: Single-Minded Surgeon." *BBC News Online,* September 2, 2001.

Leopold, L. E. *The Columbia Encyclopedia.* Edition 6. New York: Columbia University Press, 2000, p. 3527.

Maugh, Thomas, II. "Pioneer Heart Surgeon Christiaan Barnard Dies." *Los Angeles Times,* September 3, 2001, p. A1.

"Milestones." *Time,* September 17, 2001, v. 158, p. 25.

"Obituaries." *The Washington Post,* September 9, 2001, p. C-04.

Rajendran, P. "Cloning Will Play a Major Role in Surgery." Rediff on the Net.Posted 1997.

Richman, Alan. "Christiaan Barnard Endorses Cosmetics and the Famous Heart Surgeon Gets Creamed." *People Weekly,* April 14, 1986, v. 25, p. 101.

Tresniowski, Alex, Patricia B. Smith, Toula Vlahou, Ginanne Brownell, and Michael Hamlyn. "King of Hearts." *People Weekly,* September 27, 2001, p. 199.

On the Web

infotrac.galegroup.com/itw/infomark (available through most large library systems; gives access to periodicals)

www.bbc.com

www.peopleweekly.com

www.time.com

Index

animal research 33-35, 36

apartheid 14-15

Banting, Frederick   7

Baptist Medical Center   43

Barnard, Adam Hendrik   13, 15

Barnard, Andre   23, 42

Barnard, Christiaan

    birth of, 13

    childhood of,   15-18

    death of,   44

    education of,

        at UCT 21-22

        at Univ.of Minn. 25, 27-29

        at UVA 29

    general practice,   22-23

    Glycel   43

    marriage,

        to Louw, Aletta   23

        to Setzkorn, Karin   43

        to Zoellner, Barbara   42, 43

    operations,

        open heart surgery   28, 33-34

        kidney transplants   36

        heart transplants   38-39

    senior residency,   23

    work at Baptist Medical Center, 43

Barnard, Jr. Christiaan   42

Barnard, Deirdre   23

Barnard, Dodsley   17

Barnard, Frederick   42

Barnard, Johannes   17

Barnard, Marie Elisabeth   13, 16

Barnard, Marius   17, 34, 39

Calvinism   14

Carrel, Alexis   9

Darvall, Denise   37, 39

Darvall, Myrtle Ann   37

Darvall, Edward   38

Glycel   43

Groote Schuur Hospital   22, 24, 30, 33, 38

Guthrie, Charles   9

Hardy, James   36

heart-lung machine   28

J.S. Marais Research Laboratory 34

Laks, Hillel   11

Lillehei, C. Walton   27

Lollobrigidia, Gina   42

Loren, Sophia   42

Louw, Aletta   22,23

Lower, Richard R. 27-28, 36-37

Schumway, Norman   27-28, 35, 36-37, 41

Setzkorn, Karin   43

Shelley, Mary   9

Teller, Edward   7

University of Cape Town (UCT) 21, 34

Varco, Richard   27

Wangensteen, Owen H. 27, 29

Washkansky, Ann 37

Washkansky, Louis   38, 41

xeno-transplantation 36

Zoellner, Barbara 42, 43